As you can see, Dennis is a firm believer in the American custom of helping others. Here he is...the little darling... getting ready to surprise his mother. Just wait until she gets home...

Oh, well. Virtue is its own reward.

Dennis the Menace

All-American Kid

BY HANK KETCHAM

FAWCETT GOLD MEDAL • NEW YORK

DENNIS THE MENACE, ALL-AMERICAN KID

Published by Fawcett Gold Medal Books,
a unit of CBS Publications,
the Consumer Publishing Division of CBS Inc.,
by arrangement with Hank Ketcham

ISBN: 0-449-13779-1

Printed in the United States of America

23   22   21   20   19   18   17

"SURE IT'S FREE! YA THINK I'D PAY FOR MILK?"

"MISS WAGNER! DENNIS HOCUS-POCUSED MY APPLE AND NOW HE SAYS HE CAN'T *FIND* IT!"

"I THOUGHT WE CAME HERE TO *LEARN* STUFF! I ALREADY *KNOW* HOW TO SLEEP!"

"HE GOT IN A LUCKY PUNCH! HE GOT IN A *WHOLE BUNCH* OF LUCKY PUNCHES!"

"BUT I DON'T *NEED* A BATH! WHEN I TAKE OFF THESE DIRTY CLOTHES I'LL BE GOOD AS *NEW!*"

"HEY, YA WANNA KNOW SOMETHIN'? I'M TALLER
SITTIN' DOWN THAN I AM *STANDIN' UP!*"

"GEE WHIZ! I DON'T PUSH *YOU* OUTSIDE EVERTIME YOU GET ON *MY* NERVES!"

"AFTER THIS, HONEY, JUST SAY "GOODBYE."
YOU DON'T HAVE TO TELL HIM TO "BE GOOD.""

"SEE? LEATHER ON THE OUTSIDE, SILK ON THE INSIDE, AN' A REAL LOCK AN' KEY. ISN'T THAT A *PERFECT* BOX FOR KEEPIN' ROCKS IN?"

"IF YOU'RE BORED, WE COULD ALWAYS MAKE FUDGE!"

"Yeah, she's got a *LOT* of knives. She's part *PIRATE*, y'know!"

"DID YOU *HAVE* TO SAY WE WERE GOING TO THE POOR FARM?
HE'S UPSTAIRS *PACKING!*"

"...AN' THEN HE SAYS, 'LOOK AT *THESE BILLS!*' AN'
THEN HE CHEWS ON HIS FINGERNAILS SOME MORE."

"IT WAS THE WRONG NUMBER, DAD.
SOME GUY WANTED TO SPEAK TO MR......HEY! THAT'S *YOUR* NAME!"

"I CAN'T COME OUT, DEWEY. I'M SICK!"

"IT'S CALLED 'BROTH', JOEY. IT'S LIKE *EMPTY SOUP!*"

"HERE'S THE *BIG* GYP: I HAVEN'T BEEN OUTA THE HOUSE IN THREE WHOLE DAYS, AN' I *STILL* HADDA TAKE A *BATH!*"

"YA KNOW SOMETHIN', MARGARET? I'M SO DARN LONESOME I'M EVEN GLAD TO SEE *YOU!*"

"OPEN THIS DOOR OR I'LL BREAK IT DOWN!"

"GEE WHIZ, I *SAID* 'HA-HA'!"

"YOU SURE GOT A NICE VOICE, WHEN YOU'RE NOT YELLIN' AT ME."

"IF IT'S HEADS, YOU GIVE ME A SODA; AN' IF IT'S TAILS, I'LL LEAVE. YOU GOT A PENNY? ....."

"YES, HE WAS IN HERE. HE HAD A GLASS OF WATER, TIPPED OVER A JAR OF STRAWS, TOOK A HANDFUL OF NAPKINS, AND LEFT."

"WE'RE JUST GONNA LOOK AROUND AN' SEE
IF ANYBODY DROPPED ANY MONEY."

"Gee, I wouldn't mind takin' tap dancin' if I could have some *NOISY* shoes like those!"

"WHY, I NEVER KNEW YOUR FATHER WAS A SAILOR! THE OL' *RASCAL!*"

"AN' THEY ALL GOT NAMES. THERE'S THE BIG FLIPPER, AN' THAT'S MR. O'BRIAN'S BELT, AN'......"

"...AN' IT WAS *HOT!* AN' ALL I COULD SEE WAS *SAND*...FILL 'ER UP AGAIN....AN' *CACTUS* AN'....."

"I TRIED THAT ONCE. BUT THE BACK OF MY MOUTH *LEAKS!*"

"COULD I HAVE MY HOTCAKES IN A BOWL? I LIKE *LOTS* OF SYRUP!"

"MAYBE MR. BAKER CAN PLAY WITH ME. HE'S A *BACHELOR!*"

"But you shouldn't get mad just because Kenny said that. I *AM* lanky!"

"WANNA HEAR A POEM MY DAD MADE UP ABOUT BARBERS? 'CLIP, CLIP, SCISSORS AN' SNIP; SPARE MY EAR AN' BUTTON YOUR LIP!'"

"HENRY! WILL YOU COME UP HERE? ONE OF DENNIS' BUREAU DRAWERS IS *HISSING* AT ME!"

"SOME OF THIS FURNITURE IS *REAL* OLD. WE EVEN HAD THIS CHAIR BEFORE I WAS *BORN!*"

"COME ON, BEAUTIFUL! DINNER'S READY."

"HE NEEDS GLASSES MORE THAN SHE DOES!"

"THAT'S FUNNY. MR. WILSON *HEARD* YA CALLIN' ME!"

"MR. WILSON HAS A *RIGHT* TO TELL ME WHEN YOU'VE BEEN NAUGHTY. BUT YOU *DON'T* HAVE A RIGHT TO CALL HIM A "BIG MOUTH"!"

"GEE, MOM! CAN'T YOU PLAY HOUSE SOME *OTHER* TIME?"

"HEY, MOM! I THINK MY FEET ARE GETTIN' FARTHER AWAY!"

"I'M TOO *HUNGRY* FOR GRAPES! I WANT SOMETHIN' *FASTER!*"

"CAKE WOULDN'T SPOIL MY APPETITE! IT'S CARROTS AN' JUNK THAT SPOIL MY APPETITE!"

"NOW WE'LL JUST *SEE* IF HE'D RATHER STARVE DEAD THAN EAT THEM LOUSY OL' CARROTS!"

"WHY CAN'T HE SLEEP IN THE BEDROOM? THIS IS THE *LIVIN'* ROOM!"

"THAT'S WHAT I THINK OF YOU! AND HERE'S WHAT I THINK OF YOUR GOOFY DOG..." 'MOTHER!'

"GEE, HOW CAN YA PAINT A PICTURE WITHOUT ANY LITTLE NUMBERS TO GO BY?"

"BOY, I'M *POOPED!* I BEEN LOOKIN'
UNDER ROCKS *ALL MORNIN'!*"

"IT'S LIKE A GREAT BIG PHONOGRAPH RECORD, WITH HORSES ON IT, AN' YA SIT ON A HORSE WHILE IT PLAYS MUSIC. *THAT'S* A MERRY-GO-ROUND!"

"WHAT TIME IS SHE GONNA TRY AN' PUT ME TO BED?"

"YOU SHOULDA BEEN A DETECTIVE! YOU'RE ALWAYS LOOKIN' FOR *FINGER PRINTS!*"

"WHEN I SAY "CAN WE HAVE A COOKIE?", SAY "YES". JOEY'S GOT EASY HURT FEELINGS."

"SURE I'M USING GLUE. YOU WOULDN'T WANT THE WALL FULL OF *NAIL HOLES*, WOULD YA?"

"OPEN IT SLOW. HE MAY BE ALL READY TO JUMP!"

"YOU DON'T MEAN YOU 'BROKE UP THE PARTY EARLY', YOU MEAN 'THE PARTY BROKE UP EARLY!'" "DON'T YOU?"

"DON'T PEOPLE EVER GIVE *CANDY*
WHEN THEY HAVE NEW BABIES?"

"THIS IS WHERE I KEEP MY TOYS . . . . . IF I DON'T WANNA
BE YELLED AT."

"I'M NOT GONNA GO TO BED, SEE?"

"WANNA SHAKE? I'M A GOOD LOSER."

"*FOOLED* YA, DIDN'T I? I'LL BET YOU THOUGHT I WAS A *REAL* ROOSTER!"

"DON'T YOU 'MEMBER *LAST* TIME? WE SPENT
'BOUT AN <u>HOUR</u> IN THOSE SANDPILES!"

"HE MAY LIKE GOLF, BUT HE *HATES* THAT LITTLE BALL!"

"OH, *HI*, DAD! YOU WANNA USE THE BOAT HARBOR?"

"LOOK AT THIS! HE'S BEEN SAVING ORANGE PEELINGS, SO MRS. WILSON CAN MAKE HIM SOME MORE MARMALADE!"

"YES, MA'AM, I KNOW WHERE IT IS. IT'S OUT IN THE SUN GETTIN' RID OF A ROOT BEER SPOT."

"YOU SURE GOT MRS. WILSON FOOLED. SHE THINKS YOU'RE *SWEET!*"

"YOU KNOW HOW YOU KEEP SAYING WE SHOULD LIVE CLOSER TO OUR GRANDCHILDREN, TOM? WELL, *FORGET* IT!"

"I'VE BEEN NERVOUS AS A CAT. HE KEPT OPENING DOORS AND SHOOTING BURGLARS *ALL EVENING!*"

"BOY, THIS IS FUN! UNTIL MY MOM WALKS IN."

"GEE, I DON'T KNOW WHY JUST *ME* WOULD MAKE YA SO TIRED. NOW, IF YOU WAS THE OL' LADY WHO LIVED IN A SHOE...."

"...AN' IF THE NEIGHBORS GET *REALLY* SORE AT YA, TAKE A NAP. THEN YA CAN'T BE DISTURBED."

"YOU WERE RIGHT. IT'S BAD LUCK TO OPEN AN UMBRELLA IN THE HOUSE. YA GET *SHOUTED* AT!"

"HE'S BEEN SINGING 'POLLY WOLLY DOODLE' ALL THE DAY. AND I MEAN *ALL THE DAY!*"

"YOU SAID 'A COUPLE OF PUFFS'. YOU STILL HAVE ONE COMING."

"BUT ALL I WANT IS A PIECE OF BREAD WITH A LITTLE PEANUT BUTTER ON IT. AN' SOME JELLY. AN' A FEW RAISINS ....."

"COULD YOU SHOW JOEY YOUR SNAKESKIN BELT? HE'S 'FRAID OF SNAKES, BUT HE'S PRETTY BRAVE AROUND BELTS."

"YOU SURE GOT A NICE BATHROOM. BUT WHO WAS THAT LADY BEHIND THE TOWEL?"

"WHY IS SHORT GRASS BETTER'N LONG GRASS?"

"...THAT'S TOMMY, THAT'S BILLY, AN' THAT'S JOEY.
AN' WE'RE *ALL BROKE!*"

"Joey's cryin' 'cause Ruff gave him a kiss THIS LONG!"

"DID YA HEAR *THAT*? HE SAYS RUFF IS A *REAL* MIXTURE!"

"HIS NAME IS ALFRED. I THINK HE CAME
OVER TO HAVE BREAKFAST WITH RUFF."

"I CAN'T TAKE HIM BACK! I ALREADY *ADAPTED* HIM!"

"IT'S A SWELL GAME. NO MATTER *WHO* WINS, ME AN' DAD ALWAYS GET A *TV DINNER!*"

"LOOK WHAT I FOUND UNDER A *ROCK!*"

"YOU'LL BE SORRY WHEN PEOPLE SAY 'HOW'S YOUR MOTHER?' AN' I SAY 'MEAN!'"

"TAKE YOUR TIME. DON'T FALL FOR THE FIRST UGLY FACE YA SEE!"

"BOY! JOEY'S REALLY *HAPPY*! HE SCARED
TWO BIG PEOPLE AN'A BLACK DOG!"

"IT WOULDN'T BE SO TERRIBLE IF THAT THING WHERE THE TEA COMES OUTA THE TEAPOT WAS A LITTLE *SHORTER*, WOULD IT?"

"DON'T SAY 'AIN'T', JOEY!"

"AW, MARGARET, HE AREN'T *OLD* ENOUGH TO TALK GOOD LIKE US!"

"BUT I DIDN'T SAY 'STICK 'EM UP!' HE SAID 'STICK 'EM UP!'!"

"CUT IT REAL SHORT AN' PAINT IT BLACK."

"I SURE DON'T UNDERSTAND MOM. SHE SAYS WHEN I SIT HERE I'M *HELPING* HER!"

"I COULD SHOW YA HOW TO GET *MILLIONS* OF 'EM FOR *NOTHIN'*...
IF YA DON'T MIND A LITTLE YELLIN'."

"COFFEE IS SOMETHIN' YOUR PARENTS GOTTA HAVE BEFORE YOU CAN MAKE ANY NOISE IN THE MORNING."

"MOM, COULD WE BUY SOME SAGEBRUSH FOR THE BACK YARD?"

"IF THAT MAN AT THE NURSERY FOUND SOME SHOES AN' SOCKS BY HIS FISHPOND, HE'D *SAVE* 'EM, WOULDN'T HE?"

"YES, HE'S HERE, MR. MITCHELL. BUT HE DOESN'T WISH TO SEE YOU."

"AN' DON'T CALL ME 'PAL' NO MORE! YA DON'T MAKE A 'PAL' SIT IN A LOUSY OL' *CORNER!*"

"YOU FORGOT TO SAY 'GO TO BED', AN' I'M *SLEEPY!*"

"I DIDN'T LIKE THE SITTER YA LEFT ME WITH!"

"HE THINKS HE *KNOWS* YOUR COAT!"

"I'LL STOP RUNNIN' UP 'N DOWN THE AISLES IF *YOU'LL*
TELL ME WHERE YOU KEEP YOUR *BATHROOM!*"

"I COULD HEAR THE LAUGHS, BUT I WAS MISSIN' THE *JOKES!*"

"MR. WILSON! HERE'S A PICTURE OF ME TO KEEP IN YOUR WALLET!"

"IF YOU THINK *I* SLAM DOORS, YOU OUGHTA HEAR MR. WILSON SEND ME HOME SOMETIME!"

"WHICH MR. MITCHELL DID YA WANNA TALK TO?
THE TALL ONE OR THE SHORT ONE?"

"I HAVTA SCRAPE SOME JELLY OFF MY BEDROOM CEILING."

"HEY! ARE WE OUTA *CATSUP*?"

"IT'S NOT FAIR TO WHAM MY PANTS AN'
THEN MAKE ME *SIT* ON 'EM!"

"I DON'T KNOW *WHAT* TO HAVE FOR DINNER."

"... AN' CHILI, AN' A HOTDOG, AN' CHOCLATE CAKE AN' A GLASS OF ROOTBEER! HOW'S *THAT* SOUND?"

"YEAH, BUT LOOK AT MY *HANDS!* LOOK AT MY *HANDS!*"

"YOU WOULDN'T WANT ME TO FALL DOWN AN' GET HURT WHILE I'M JUST TRYIN' TO GET SOME COOKIES, WOULD YOU?"

"MARGARET WANTS TO KNOW THE SIZE OF THAT BABY BIRD DENNIS FOUND. IS IT TEENY, TEENY-WEENY, OR TEENY-WEENY-EENY?"

"BOY, I'LL NEVER SHAKE HANDS WITH A *PARROT* AGAIN!"

"MMMM, BOY! WHAT THE HECK *SMELLS* SO GOOD, JOEY?"

"YOU MEAN WE *STILL* DON'T WEIGH A HUNDRED POUNDS?"

"COULD YOU PACK ME A LUNCH? ONCE I START A HOLE I LIKE TO STAY THERE 'TIL IT'S FINISHED!"

"DON'T LOOK IN THE CLOSET 'TIL I GET 'EM BACK IN THEIR BOX!"

"HI, MOM! DAD FINALLY PUT *ONE* OF US TO SLEEP!"

"I'LL BET HE'S DREAMING ABOUT ME. HE JUST MUMBLED 'I DON'T *WANNA*!'"